All From Love

Terrence Rushton

BookLeaf Publishing
India | USA | UK

Presentation by *BookLeaf Publishing*

Web: www.bookleafpub.com

E-mail: info@bookleafpub.com

ISBN : 9789357447300

First edition 2021

DEDICATION

Dedicated to my loving family. Our memories
have inspired these words.

PREFACE

Sometimes the way we remember the journey is more important than where we end up.

Across the miles

I write you tonight, with your kiss on my lips
And your body still warm on my mind,
I write you this poem, to thank you my darling
For being my shoulder in time.

I still feel your kiss and the closeness of you,
As we parted and said our goodbyes.
And I give you this love that I feel in my heart
And the love that I can see in your eyes.

And for all of this time, time we spend far apart
Our love will bridge all the miles,
My body is aching and my heart will yearn
That I can see one of your smiles.

Let time be the judge of my feelings for you
And you, of your feelings for me
For I feel in my heart, and I know that it's true
That you are the woman for me.

And so as I close I will say to you now
And still, as I thank god above
These feelings for you that I have in my heart
Are truly, most beautiful love.

My girl

For I know in my heart, and I feel in my soul
And I see in the stars up above
When I look in the sky, I picture your face
And I know in my heart I'm in love.

Yes you are my girl, you are just right for me
And so it is etched in my soul
The love of my life, you will always be
My girl, my darling, my all.

Yes I love you so much that words cannot tell
How my mind can reach such a high,
Just to hear you speak and to know you are there
And to know that I'm on your mind.

Yes you have my heart and you have my love
And so you have all my trust
My darling my Lezah, you'll be my love
As ashes to ashes and dust is to dust.

I'm all yours

Why do I dream my sweetest dreams
Whenever I dream of you
And why do I smile my brightest smiles
And love you the way that I do.

Why is it that this heart of mine
Is happy and so full of joy
And why do I miss you when you are not here
And the love that I see in your eyes

Why do I know that I've never been
In love like this before
For now I can tell just how good that I feel
And I'm loving you more and more.

I need to be with you and hold you so tight
To be happy and warm in your arms
And I need to be with you and know it's so right
And not have to leave you again.

With all of these things that I've said to you now
With all of those things left to say
Please know that my love is yours all alone
And this is a love time won't fade away.

Say goodbye as you leave me tonight

Say goodbye softly as you leave me tonight
Just tell me you love me and turn out the light
And remember the places we've been and the
things we have seen
Tonight as we floated through our special dream.

Tonight you have held me tight to your breast
And laid here besides me and loved me the best
Yes, we were together, as forever we'll be
And the past will become just an old memory.

Tonight you have given me hope for all time
This I know that your love and trust are mine
For tonight you have shown me how dearly you
care
I love you my darling and I know you'll be there.

So say goodbye softly as you leave me tonight
And wipe away gently the tears from our eyes
Be happy my darling, be glad and be free
And know that I love you for I know you love
me!

Wishing

I wish to be beside you
At the breaking of the dawn
When the birds begin their singing
And the dew sets on the lawn
I'd love to be beside you
At the start of each new day
As the sunlight brightens up the room
And warms you where you lay

And I'd love to be there with you
And just not have to care
Whether someone else had seen us
Or knew that I was there
I'd love to be beside you
And hold you close and tight
And watch the morning pass away
And welcome back the night.

When you had to leave

I was lonely last night when you had to leave
Lonely for you, so lonely it seems
That I know I'm so happy and I trust and believe
That you'll always be with me and you'll share
my dreams.

But I know that sometimes, you'll have to go
Homeward again, homeward to rest
Away from my loving, and so you must know
That of the good things in life, I love you the
best.

And so I know that I'll see you again
And hold you and touch you and treasure your
smile
And know that our love will hold us together
Forever my darling, not just for a while.

Sparkle of love

I see in your eyes, that sparkle of love
As bright and as pretty as the stars up above
And there on your lips that warm happy smile
That tells me our love is good and worthwhile.

Yes we have a good love, so special and deep
A fine love, a bright love, a love we will keep
So please love me tomorrow as you love me still
And we'll stay together, forever, we will.

Today is the start

It is time like today, when you are not here
When I can't see your smile, and I can't hold
your hand
That I miss you the most, and I love you so dear
And I pray that the others, will, one day,
understand.

For how can they know, what I feel in my heart
And how can they know all the times that I've
cried
And they will never know how it tore me apart
To live through those years as I died deep inside.

So just hold me close and let your love shine
And hug me and kiss me and tell me you care
And know that I want you to always be mine
For today is the start of the future we'll share.

So Lezah please know that I love you so dear
And know that inside, once more I'm alive
And know that tomorrow and forever we'll be
in love with each other and together for life.

To be there beside you

To have you here with me is all that I wish
To hold you and love you and kiss your sweet
lips
To see your warm smile and feel your soft touch
To be away for one hour is one hour too much.

I miss you my darling and I'll hurry home
To be there beside you - no longer alone
And I'll hold you close and I'll hold you tight
And love you forever, not just for a night.

So wait for me darling for soon I'll be there
To tell you I love you to tell you I care
To lay there beside you and look in your eyes
And fall asleep slowly just watching your smile.

Together we'll be

I'm sitting here waiting to see your sweet smile
And hold you close in my arms for a while
Knowing that soon, beside you I'll be
Because I'm missing you and you're missing me.

I gather my strength in the arms of my love
And I give you my body, my soul and my trust
And with you I know just how great love can be
For I know for the future, together we'll be.

To my future wife

You know I love your smoothness and your
softness and your love
And I love to be beside you and pleasure in your
touch
And I remember times when I've looked up in
surprise
And found the world a nicer place for the
sparkle in your eyes.

And you know that your beauty is all that I see
And your kisses and laughter are there just for
me
And I take pleasure and comfort in your arms
and your touch
And for being here with me, I love you so much.

And I love to spend my afternoons and nights
alone with you
And have you close, and hold you tight, and love
you like I do
To share with you my hopes and dreams and
plan our future life
And know that soon you'll always be, my lover
and my wife.

My thoughts are of you

It's days like today when flowers bloom bright
When I can't be with you till day turns to night
That I miss you the most, and yes I feel blue
So I turn to my thought and my thoughts are of
you.

And I wish you were here with me, your head on
my chest
Your eyes gently closed, a sweet smile on your
face
Yes I wish you were with me, and if so I'd say
That my love will grow stronger, day after day.

Hold me close

Hold me close darling, cling to me tight
Tell me you love me and stay for the night
Just lie here beside me sleep safe in my arms
With your head on my chest and your heart in
my heart.

Sleep gently my darling till morn when we wake
And hold my love dearly, it's your just to take
Be free with your smiles, for they light your
eyes
And lay here all morning and greet the sunrise.

Be comfortable darling in knowing my love
Be confident too and give me your trust
Be happy and carefree and gentle and kind
And give me your love as I give you mine.

Welcome my love

Welcome home my darling
There's that sparkle in your eyes
Come fill our home with beauty, your beauty,
The kind that money couldn't buy.

Come hold me close my darling
The way you always do
Come brighten up my day again
And feel this love, the love so true.

Come kiss me now my darling
And hug me close and tight
For I know that now you're here
Everything's alright.

Come look me in the eyes my love
And let your beauty shine
Please know I'm happy that you're home
To share this love of mine.

The birth of our first son

How can I thank you for what we've become
More words cannot say how I feel
I held your hand tightly through all of your pain
I sat there beside you to conquer your fears.
Every breath, every pain, every fear that you felt
I felt in my heart and I shared all your tears,
Till morningtime came and you hold forth our
son
And I watched you with pride as you hold him
so near
For all time I'll remember that look in your eyes
And the love that flowed forth from your heart.
And you hold our dear son so close to your
breast
And forgot all the pain that gave life this start.

Before you came home

I sit here tonight with the taste of your lips
And the warmth of your touch on my mind
I sit here my darling to write you this verse
And give you my love till the end of my life

I can see in my mind the love in your smile
And the long golden locks of your hair
I miss you my darling and wish you were here
For to be here without you no more can I bear.

I long for tomorrow when you shall come home
And you'll bear in your arms our new son
Oh so happy again and together we'll be
Forever a family ....the past is now gone.

Yes I welcome tomorrow and the rest of our
lives
And I welcome the love that we share
No one could imagine how happy I feel
To know that tomorrow, again you'll be there.

Emily - Child of sunshine

Oh Emily child of sunshine
You came to our world
With eyes so bright
A sweet little pearl
Our little girl
You fill our hearts with delight

Emily's wedding

This started as a speech, then it turned into a
story.
It's a tale of love and friendship between Emily
and Rory.
We all knew that it would work out, we all saw it
from the start;
And we never, ever doubted that Rory held Em's
heart.

At times she thought the navy was conspiring to
keep them both apart.
However, distance wouldn't beat them, they
were soul mates from the start.
So they would drive, or take the bus to see each
other, from their current posts,
Just to spend special time together with the one
they loved the most.

Long hours spent on work and study, stolen
moments in between,
Away in Cooma – off to Sale, back in Canberra
– off to sea!
Resilience, determination, lots of travel, they
kept it well in hand,

Overseas deployments, back to dockside, feet
now planted back on land.

Though, they lived in different cities, special
moments still they shared.
Then, on a special trip to Mollymook; he
showed how much he cared,
He took her walking on the beach, and, on one
knee in the sand;
Like the gentleman he has always been, he asked
her for her hand.

So to their different cities Em and Rory did
return,
till the navy finally decided that they would post
him back to her,
Graduations and promotions, placements, now a
home together,
Today a marriage before us all, we all know it is
forever.

And here they are before you, smiling, sitting
side by side,
An Officer and Gentleman with a Doctor as his
bride.

Our family is complete

We knew there was another little voice just
waiting to be heard,
So we tried our best to find him and bring him to
this world.
Then, after many years of trying, we had a
stroke of luck.
The stars aligned, and he was born, delightful,
happy Brock!
A kind and gentle, caring boy, his happiness is
infectious,
His smile can light the darkest night, he truly is
most precious.
A joy to be around, he is considerate and sweet,
And now that he is here with us our family is
complete.